Geometry and Fractions

From the Read-Aloud Anthology

Four Shapes

by Katherine Mead
illustrated by Nancy Coffelt

Access Prior Knowledge

This poem will help you review

- Plane shapes
- Patterns

ISBN: 0-618-671781

Printed in the U.S.A.

123456789- WC - 14 13 12 11 10 09 08 07 06 05

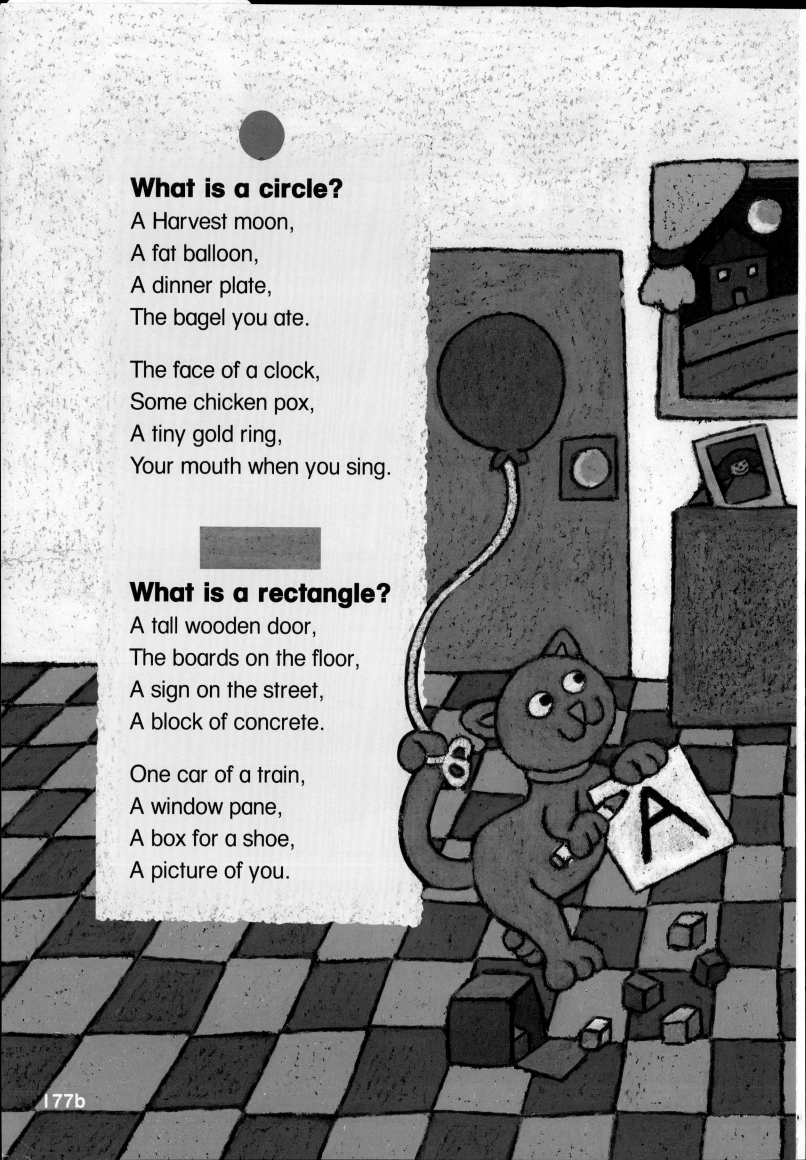

What is a circle?

A Harvest moon,
A fat balloon,
A dinner plate,
The bagel you ate.

The face of a clock,
Some chicken pox,
A tiny gold ring,
Your mouth when you sing.

What is a rectangle?

A tall wooden door,
The boards on the floor,
A sign on the street,
A block of concrete.

One car of a train,
A window pane,
A box for a shoe,
A picture of you.

What is a triangle?

The roof of a house,
The ear of a mouse,
The top of an A
When you print a neat way.

The nose of a cat,
An old soldier's hat,
An instrument made
For a rhythm parade.

What is a square?

Some buttons on coats,
Some cards and some notes,
A picture frame,
A place for a name.

One side of a box,
The shape of some blocks,
A part of a door,
The tiles on the floor.

177c

Name _____

Solve.

1. The poem tells about many things that are the shape of circles, rectangles, and triangles. Draw a pattern using all three shapes.

2. What things do you have at home that have the same shape as a circle, a triangle, and a rectangle? Draw an item for each shape.

Circle	Triangle	Rectangle

Complete the sentence.

3. A triangle has _____ sides.

4. A rectangle has _____ sides.

5. **Create Your Own** Draw a picture using triangles, circles, and rectangles.

Dear Family,

My class is starting Unit 3. I will be learning about geometry and fractions. These pages show what I will learn and have activities for us to do together.

From, _____

Vocabulary

These are some words I will use in this unit.

side   The straight part of a shape

corner   The point where sides meet

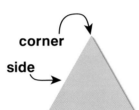

symmetry   If a figure can be folded in half and the two parts match, it has symmetry.

fraction   A fraction names part of a whole.
$\frac{1}{2}$ names each part of this circle.

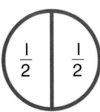

equal parts   The parts that are the same size

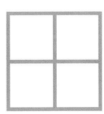

Some other words I may use are **halves**, **thirds**, **fourths**, and the names for plane and solid shapes.

Vocabulary Activity

Let's work together to complete these sentences.

1. A folded figure with two parts that match has _____ .

2. Parts that are the same size are called _____ .

3. A _____ is where the sides meet.

Turn the page for more.

How To show equal parts and fractions

This is an example of what I will be learning.

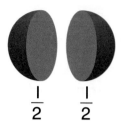

If a sphere is cut into 2 equal parts, each part is $\frac{1}{2}$ (one half) of the whole sphere.

One half ($\frac{1}{2}$) is a fraction of the whole sphere.

$$\frac{1}{2} \qquad \frac{1}{2}$$

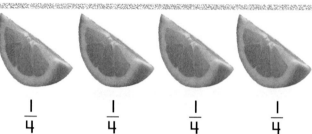

If an orange is divided into 4 equal parts, each part is $\frac{1}{4}$ (one fourth) of the whole orange.

One fourth ($\frac{1}{4}$) is a fraction of the whole orange.

$$\frac{1}{4} \qquad \frac{1}{4} \qquad \frac{1}{4} \qquad \frac{1}{4}$$

If a paper is folded into 3 equal parts, each part is $\frac{1}{3}$ of the whole paper.

One third ($\frac{1}{3}$) is a fraction of the whole paper.

$$\frac{1}{3} \qquad \frac{1}{3} \qquad \frac{1}{3}$$

Literature

These books link to the math in this unit. We can look for them at the library.

Eating Fractions by Bruce McMillan (Scholastic Trade, 1991)

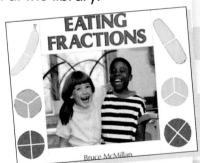

Let's Fly a Kite by Stuart Murphy

The Doorbell Rang by Pat Hutchins

Let's read together!

Education Place

We can visit *Education Place* at

eduplace.com/maf

for the Math Lingo game, *e*•Glossary, and more games and activities to do together.

Plane and Solid Shapes

CHAPTER 7

INVESTIGATION

Name the plane shapes you see in the picture.

Toy Shelf

Listen to your teacher.

Classifying and Sorting Objects

There are different ways to sort objects.

The shirts in each group are alike in one way.

color

shape

size

Guided Practice

Circle one way the objects are alike.

1.

Think
The color and shape are different.

color   size   shape

2.

color   size   shape

Tell how the hats are alike.
Write color, size, or shape.

3.

_____

Explain Your Thinking Describe how the objects in Exercise 3 are different.

Remember to look at all the objects in a group.

Tell how the objects are alike.
Write color, size, or shape.

1.

color

2.

_____

Use the shapes in this box.
Find the one that belongs
in the group. Draw it.

3.    _____

4.    _____

Problem Solving ▶ Reasoning

5. Sort the objects into two groups.
   Circle one group ✏.
   Circle the other group ✏.

6. **Talk About It** Explain how you sorted.

At Home Gather some toys and have your child sort them. Ask your child to explain how he or she sorted.

Plane Shapes

 Audio Tutor I / 22 Listen and Understand

Objective
Identify, describe, and compare attributes of plane shapes.

Vocabulary
side   corner
names for plane shapes

Some plane shapes have **sides** and **corners**.

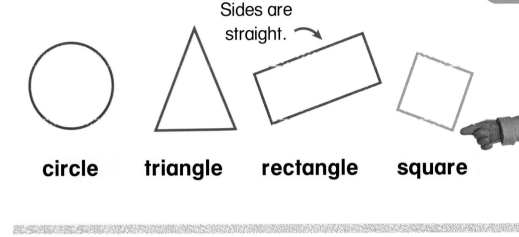

circle   triangle   rectangle   square

Corners are where the sides meet.

Guided Practice

Trace the shape.
Write the number of sides and corners.

Think
I count 4 places where the sides meet.

1. rectangle

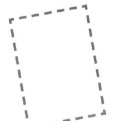

_____ sides

_____ corners

2. square

_____ sides

_____ corners

3. triangle

_____ sides

_____ corners

4. circle

_____ sides

_____ corners

Explain Your Thinking Compare the number of corners and the number of sides for each shape. Describe what you see.

Remember the shapes.

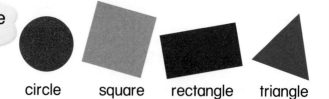

circle   square   rectangle   triangle

Answer the question.
Color the shapes on the bus.

1. How many
shapes have **0** sides? ___3___
Color the circles 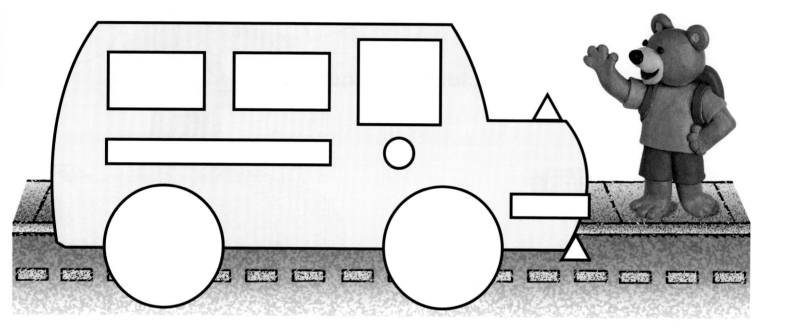.

2. How many
shapes have **3** sides? _____
Color the triangles .

3. How many shapes
have **4** sides the same? _____
Color the squares .

4. What do we call the
shapes that are not colored?

_____

Color them .

Reading Math ▶ Vocabulary

Draw the shape to match the word.

5.   circle   square   triangle   rectangle

At Home Ask your child to show you objects in your house that have
the same shape as a circle, a triangle, a rectangle, and a square.

Classifying and Sorting Shapes

Objective
Classify and sort plane shapes.

There are many ways to sort shapes.

Shapes with corners   **Shapes with 3 sides**   **Shapes with 4 corners**

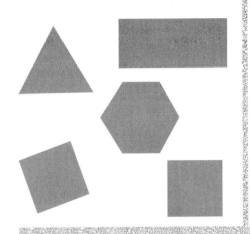  

Guided Practice

Read the sorting rule.
Circle the shapes that follow the rule.

1. **4** corners

Think
Corners are where the sides meet.

2. **4** sides the same

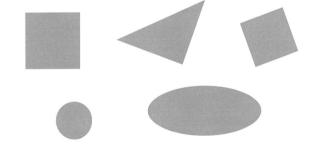

3. More than **3** sides

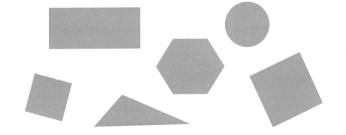

4. No corners

Explain Your Thinking How could you sort the shapes in Exercise 4 another way?

Remember to read the sorting rule first.

Read the sorting rule.
Circle the shapes that follow the rule.

1. Small shapes

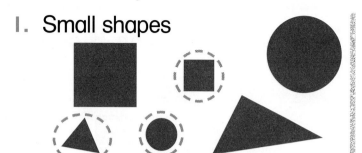

2. No corners

3. **3** corners

4. More than **2** sides

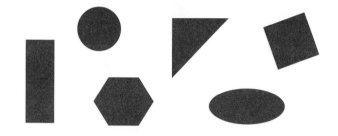

Write a sorting rule.
Draw **3** shapes that follow your rule.

5. _____

_____

Problem Solving ▶ Visual Thinking

open figures   **closed figures**

Circle each open figure.
Color inside each closed figure.

6.

 At Home Gather some household objects such as photos, coins, and napkins. Ask your child to sort them by shape or size.

Go on ➡

Name_____

Sort by Two Attributes

Sometimes we use more than one sorting rule to make a set.

Small and yellow

Circle the figure that follows the rule.

1. Big and yellow

2. Round and blue

3. Open and red

Use the figures in the box. Find and draw the figure that follows the rule.

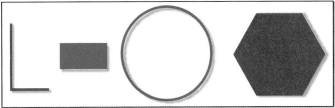

4. Small and blue

5. Closed and red

6. **Talk About It** How did you choose figures for Exercises 4 and 5?

Tell how the balls are alike.
Write color, size, or shape.

1.

_____

Trace the shape.
Write how many sides and corners.

2. rectangle

_____ sides

_____ corners

3. triangle

_____ sides

_____ corners

Read the sorting rule.
Circle the shapes that follow the rule.

4. No corners

Circle the figure that follows the rule.

5. Small and red

Facts Practice, see page 669

Name_____

Activity: Solid Shapes

 Audio Tutor I/23 Listen and Understand

Objective
Identify, describe, and compare solid shapes.

Vocabulary
names for solid shapes
face   edge   corner

Solid shapes have special names.

cube   **cone**   **cylinder**

rectangular prism   **pyramid**   **sphere**

Work Together

Find how each solid can move.
Complete the table.

		Slide	Stack	Roll
1.		yes	no	yes
2.				
3.				
4.				

5. **Talk About It** Use the words **round**, **flat**, **curved**, and **straight** to describe the shapes you used.

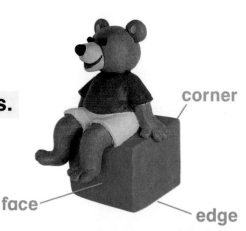

Work Together

Some solids have **faces**, **edges**, and **corners.**
Work with a partner to complete the table.
Use solid shapes. Start with a cube.

	Name of Solid	Number of Faces	Number of Edges	Number of Corners
1.	cube	6	12	8
2.	rectangular prism			
3.	pyramid			
4.	sphere			

On Your Own

Circle the solid that matches.

5. **I** face

Use your shapes to help you.

6. **12** edges

7. **8** corners

8. **Talk About It** Tell how a pyramid and a cube are alike and different.

 At Home Ask your child to find an object in your house that will slide, stack, and roll.

Classifying and Sorting Solid Shapes

Objective
Classify and sort solid shapes.

There are many ways to sort solid shapes.

 **6 faces**   **Curved parts**   **8 corners**

Guided Practice

Read the sorting rule.
Circle the solid shapes that follow the rule.

1. All faces

Think
The cup and cone have curved parts.

2. Roll

3. Has edges

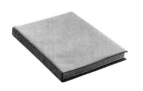

Explain Your Thinking Tell how the solid shapes in Exercise 2 are alike and different.

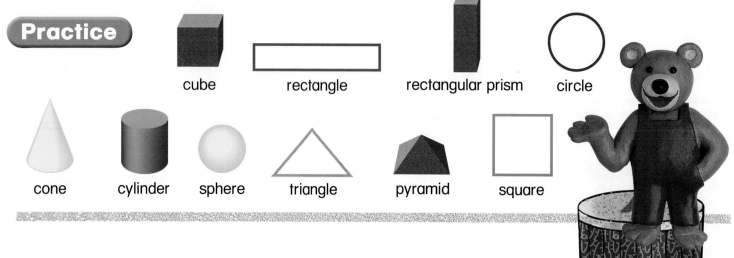

cube   rectangle   rectangular prism   circle

cone   cylinder   sphere   triangle   pyramid   square

Use the sorting rule to sort the shapes.

Draw the shape or write the name.

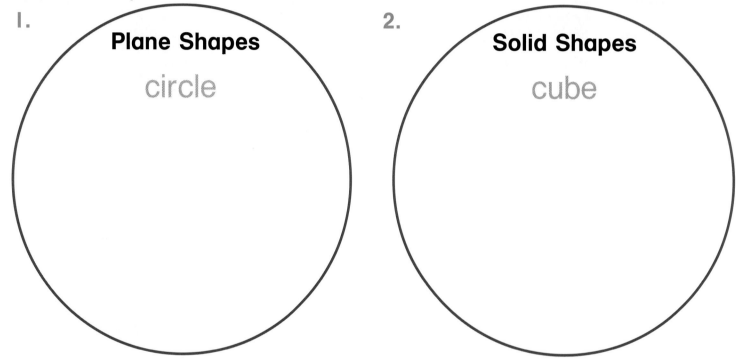

1.

Plane Shapes

circle

2.

Solid Shapes

cube

Problem Solving ▶ Reasoning

3. Sort the solid shapes into two groups.
   Color one group .
   Color one group .
   Explain your sorting rule.

_____

_____

At Home Have your child choose a solid shape and find things in your home that are the same shape.

Name_____

Identify Faces of a Solid Shape

 Audio Tutor 1/24 Listen and Understand

Objective
Identify the faces of a solid shape.

The face of a solid is a plane shape.

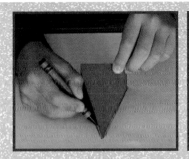   

triangle   square   rectangle   circle

Guided Practice

Look at the blue face of the solid shape.
Circle the shape of the face.

1.
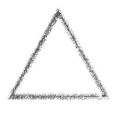
square

circle

triangle

2.

square

circle

triangle

3.

rectangle

circle

triangle

4.

square

circle

triangle

Explain Your Thinking Tell how a cylinder and a cone are alike and different.

Remember to look at all of the faces of the solids.

Look at the plane shape.
Circle the solid with a face like it.

1.

2.

3.

4.

Problem Solving ▶ Reasoning

Look at the plane shapes on each solid.
Use the plane shapes to sort the solids into two groups.
Color one group ▆▆▆.
Color the other group ▆▆▆.

5.
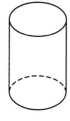 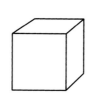  

6. **Write About It** Explain your sorting rule.

_____

_____

At Home Give your child some boxes. Have him or her trace around a face of each and tell you what plane shape was drawn.

Name_____

Draw a Picture

 Audio Tutor 1 / 25 Listen and Understand

Jane is making a picture of a boat.
She uses these shapes.

How can she make a boat?

UNDERSTAND

What do you know?

· Jane is making a boat.
· She uses these shapes.

PLAN

You can draw a picture.

Try different ways to use
the shapes.

SOLVE

Draw a picture of a boat.
Use the three shapes.

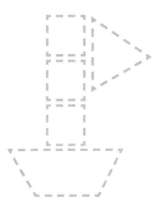

LOOK BACK

Does your answer solve the problem?
What helped you decide how to use the shapes?

Remember:
► Understand
► Plan
► Solve
► Look Back

Remember to use
the four steps.

Draw a picture to solve.

Draw or write to explain.

1. Nico wants to make a picture of a house. He uses these shapes.

How can he make a house?

Think
I start by thinking about the shape of a whole house.

2. Millie wants to make **2** triangles from this piece of paper. Draw a line to show how she can do it.

Think
A triangle has 3 sides and 3 corners.

Practice

3. Don wants to make a picture of a rocket. He uses these shapes.
How can he make a rocket?

4. Tarika wants to make **6** triangles from this shape. Draw lines to show how she can do it.

Go on

Name_____

Mixed Problem Solving

Solve.

Draw or write to explain.

1. How can Matt make
   4 triangles from this
   piece of ceramic tile?

ceramic tile

2. Sergio uses papier mâché
   to make **5** trees.
   Jill makes **4** trees.
   How many trees do
   they both make?

papier mâché

_____ trees

3. Andy makes **6** sculptures.
   He gives **2** sculptures
   to his sister. How many
   sculptures does he have
   left?

sculptures

_____ sculptures

4. **Multistep** Tony makes
   3 blue origami birds.
   Rose makes **7** red origami
   birds. They tape **6** of the
   birds to the window.
   How many birds are not
   taped to the window?

origami bird

_____ birds

At Home Cut out a square. Ask your child to cut it to make 2 new
shapes and identify the new shapes.

Problem Solving on Tests • Listening Skills

Open Response

Listen to your teacher read the problem.
Solve.

1. Rosa makes this picture of a boat. How many triangles are in the picture?

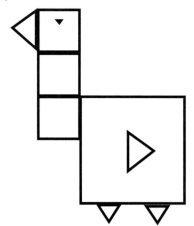

Show your work using pictures, numbers, or words.

_____ triangles

2. Jared makes this picture of a bird. What two shapes does he use to make his picture?

_____

_____

Multiple Choice

Listen to your teacher read the problem.
Choose the correct answer.

3. 1 ○   2 ○   3 ○   4 ○

4. 1 ○   2 ○   3 ○   4 ○

Education Place
See eduplace.com/map
for more Test-Taking Tips.

200 two hundred

Name_____

These plane shapes have sides and corners.

pentagon   hexagon

Trace the shape.

Write the number of sides and corners.

1. hexagon

_____ sides

_____ corners

2. pentagon

_____ sides

_____ corners

Draw the shape to match the word.

3.
	pentagon	hexagon

Social Studies Connection
Keys

People have been using keys for a long time. Keys are used to keep things safe. They come in many shapes and sizes.

Circle one way the keys are the same.

color

size

shape

Talk About It What do you think the key at the top could open?

WEEKLY WR READER eduplace.com/map

Key Topic Review
Subtraction Through 10

Write the difference.

1. $10 - 4 = \underline{\hspace{1cm}}$ 2. $9 - 2 = \underline{\hspace{1cm}}$ 3. $7 - 5 = \underline{\hspace{1cm}}$

4. $8 - 4 = \underline{\hspace{1cm}}$ 5. $9 - 6 = \underline{\hspace{1cm}}$ 6. $8 - 5 = \underline{\hspace{1cm}}$

7. $10 - 7 = \underline{\hspace{1cm}}$ 8. $7 - 2 = \underline{\hspace{1cm}}$ 9. $9 - 5 = \underline{\hspace{1cm}}$

| 10. $\begin{array}{r} 8 \\ -3 \\ \hline \end{array}$ | 11. $\begin{array}{r} 7 \\ -4 \\ \hline \end{array}$ | 12. $\begin{array}{r} 9 \\ -3 \\ \hline \end{array}$ | 13. $\begin{array}{r} 10 \\ -\ 8 \\ \hline \end{array}$ | 14. $\begin{array}{r} 8 \\ -2 \\ \hline \end{array}$ | 15. $\begin{array}{r} 10 \\ -\ 2 \\ \hline \end{array}$ |

Extra Practice at **eduplace.com/map**

Chapter Review/Test

Vocabulary

Draw the shape to match the word.

1. **rectangle**	2. **square**	3. **circle**	4. **triangle**

Concepts and Skills

Circle one way the objects are alike.

5.

color

size

shape

Trace the shape.
Write the number of sides and corners.

6. rectangle

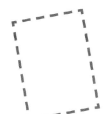

_____ sides

_____ corners

7. circle

_____ sides

_____ corners

Read the sorting rule.
Circle the shapes that follow the rule.

8. **3** corners

9. No corners

✔ Chapter Review/Test

Circle the solid that matches.

10. **2** faces

Read the sorting rule.
Circle the solid shapes that follow the rule.

11. Roll

12. All faces

Look at the blue face of the solid shape.
Circle the shape of the face.

13.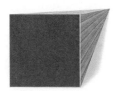

square

circle

triangle

14.

square

circle

triangle

Problem Solving

Draw a picture to solve.

15. Isabel wants to make **3** triangles from this shape. Draw lines to show how she can do it.

Draw or write to explain.

Spatial Sense and Patterns

INVESTIGATION

Use the words **inside** and **outside** to talk about the picture.

You will learn about grids in this chapter. People who plan parks use grids. Frederick Law Olmsted planned parks.

People Using Math

Frederick Law Olmsted

When Frederick Law Olmsted was a boy, he loved to be outdoors. He liked to see the wildflowers and hear the birds sing.

When Frederick went to cities, he did not see open spaces with grass and trees, or places to walk and play. He believed that everyone should have open spaces to visit.

Frederick decided to become a landscape architect, someone who plans parks. He helped create many beautiful places, like Central Park in New York City and the land around the Capitol building in Washington, D.C. His work as a park planner changed many cities.

Central Park, New York

Frederick Law Olmsted was in charge of planning Central Park until 1861. He had been in charge for 3 years. What year did he start?

Draw or write to explain.

_____

Position Words

These words tell where objects are.

Objective
Give and follow directions about position and location of objects in space.

Vocabulary
position words

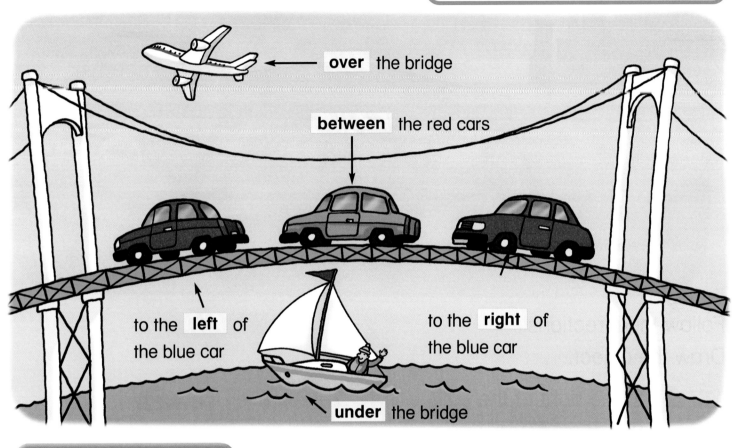

over the bridge

between the red cars

to the left of the blue car

to the right of the blue car

under the bridge

Guided Practice

Listen. Follow the directions.

I.

Explain Your Thinking Tell how you know something is to the left or to the right of you.

Follow the directions.
Draw the object.

1. to the right of the

2. ☀ over the

3. 🥁 under the

4. 🌼 to the left of the

5. Circle the objects between the 🧺 and the 🌼.

Problem Solving ▶ Logical Thinking

Use the clues to label each flower.

6. S is between B and N.
   T is to the right of B.

___ ___ ___ ___

At Home Play "I Spy." Use the words **over**, **under**, **between**, **left**, and **right** to have your child locate things you describe.

More Position Words

These words tell the location of objects.

Objective
Arrange and describe
the location of objects.

Vocabulary
position words

behind the cloud

far from the slide

In front of the sun

down the slide

next to the tree

up the ladder

near the slide

Guided Practice

Listen. Follow the directions.

1.

Explain Your Thinking Use some words from this page.
Tell how to find your desk in the classroom.

Circle the answer that completes the sentence.

1.

The ☁ is _____ the 🏢 .

⟨ in front of ⟩   behind

2.

The 🐿 goes _____ the 🌳 .

up   down

3.

The 🔴 is _____ the 🐕 .

far from   near

4.

The 🐦 is _____ the ☀ .

far from   next to

Reading Math ▶ Vocabulary

Use the word **above**, **below**, or **beside**.
Complete the sentence.

5. The rabbit is _____ the swing.

6. The butterfly is _____ the swing.

7. The flower is _____ the rabbit.

8. Draw a picture on another piece of
   paper. Use **above**, **below**, and **beside**
   to tell where things are.

At Home Have your child use words from this
lesson to describe the location of things in the kitchen.

Give and Follow Directions

Objective
Give and follow directions
to find locations on a grid.

This grid is like a map.
Follow directions to find
places in the park.

· Always start at 0.

· Go right 2 spaces.

· Then go up 4 spaces.

The ⬯ is at 2 right, 4 up.

Guided Practice

Follow the directions.
Circle to show what you find.

Think
Start at 0.
Go right 2.
Go up 2.

	Go Right	Go Up	Circle
1.	2 spaces	2 spaces	🦋 🐿️
2.	1 space	5 spaces	🌼 🌳
3.	4 spaces	1 space	🌼 🐢
4.	3 spaces	3 spaces	🐿️ ⬯

Explain Your Thinking Start at 0. Tell how to
find the tree on the grid.

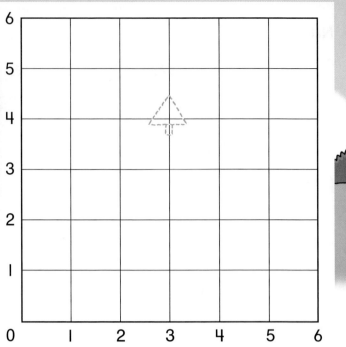

Follow the directions.
Draw an object on the grid.

Remember to start at 0.

	Go Right	Go Up	Draw
1.	3 spaces	4 spaces	🌲
2.	1 space	2 spaces	🏠
3.	4 spaces	5 spaces	〰️
4.	5 spaces	3 spaces	🚗

Problem Solving ▶ Spatial Sense

5. **Write About It** Look at the grid. Write your own directions. Tell how to get from 🏠 to 🌲.

_____

At Home Give your child directions to find places or items in your home.

Go on ➡️

Writing Math: Create and Solve

Draw items in the picture to show these words.
Label the picture with the words.

| in front |
| over |
| under |

1.

under

2. **Write About It** Tell where to draw a ☁ in your picture. Use a position word in your sentence.

_____

_____

Follow the directions.
Draw the object.

1. over the .

Circle the answer that completes the sentence.

2. The 🐕 is _____ the 🪑 .

in front of   behind

Follow the directions.
Draw an object on the grid.

	Go Right	Go Up	Draw
3.	3 spaces	3 spaces	🦋
4.	1 space	2 spaces	🐢
5.	2 spaces	1 space	🔺

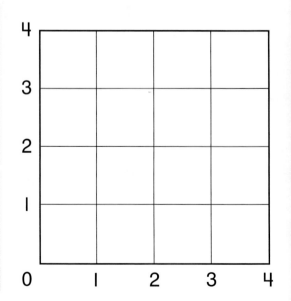

Facts Practice, see page 669

Name_____

Activity: Slides, Flips, and Turns

 Audio Tutor I / 26 Listen and Understand

Work Together

An object can be moved in different ways.
You can **flip** it, **turn** it, or **slide** it.

Work with a partner.
Use pattern blocks.
- Place the ▶ on the first shape.
- Move it to the second shape.
- Trace to show the move.

Flip ▶ to cover ◁.	Turn ▶ to cover △.	Slide ▶ to cover ▷.
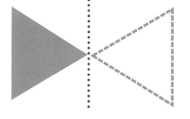	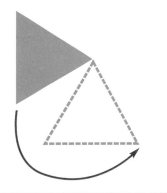	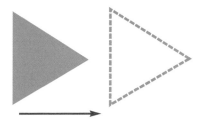

Put your block on the picture.
Pick up your block and flip it.
Then trace it.

I.

Chapter 8 Lesson 4

two hundred fifteen **215**

Put your block on the picture.
Pick up your block and flip it.
Then trace it.

1.

2.

3.

4.

Go on →

On Your Own

Put your block on the picture.
Turn your block. Then trace it.

5.

6.

7.

8.

Put your block on the picture.
Slide your block. Then trace it.

9.

10.

11.

---

12. Write About It What two moves made this picture?

_____ and _____

At Home Have your child move a book
to show a flip, a slide, or a turn.

Name_____

Patterns

 Audio Tutor I / 27 Listen and Understand

The shapes make a **pattern.**

The pattern is red, yellow, red, yellow, red, yellow.

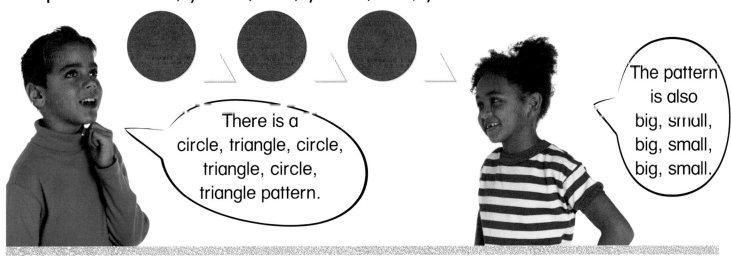

There is a circle, triangle, circle, triangle, circle, triangle pattern.

The pattern is also big, small, big, small, big, small.

Guided Practice

Use shapes to copy the pattern.
Circle the one that comes next.

1.

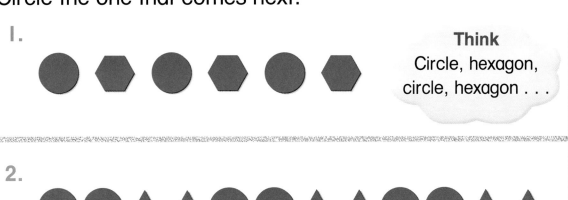

Think
Circle, hexagon, circle, hexagon . . .

2.

3.

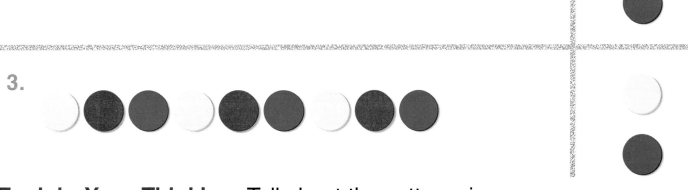

Explain Your Thinking Tell about the patterns in Exercise 1 and Exercise 3. How are they different?

Practice

Sometimes it helps to say the pattern aloud.

Use shapes to copy the pattern.
Circle the one that comes next.

1.

2.

3.

4.

Problem Solving ▶ Number Sense

Use shapes to copy the pattern.
Write the number that comes next.

5. 1 2 1 2 1 2 1 2 ____

6. 3 2 1 3 2 1 3 2 1 ____

At Home Have your child use plates, spoons, and other objects to create and describe patterns.

Name_____

Create Patterns

Kate made a pattern.

Yellow, red, blue is the pattern unit.
It repeats over and over.

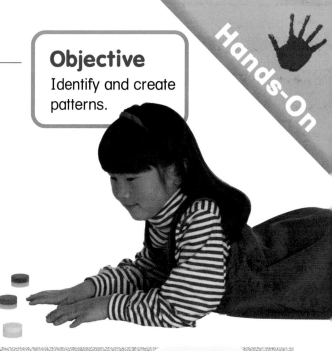

Guided Practice

Think
Circle, square, triangle repeats.

Use shapes to copy the pattern.
Circle the pattern unit.

1.

2.

Now use the shapes to make a pattern.
Draw the pattern.
Circle the pattern unit.

3.

4.

Explain Your Thinking How can you use sound to copy your pattern?

Make a pattern unit.
Then repeat it.

Use any shapes to make a pattern.
Draw the pattern.

1.

2.

3.

4. Make a number pattern. Have a friend tell what
   number might come next.

Algebra Readiness ▶ Patterns

Circle the pattern unit.
Draw the shape that comes next.

5.

6.

At Home Invite your child to make a pattern with
coins. Then have your child identify the pattern unit.

Translate Patterns

There is more than one way to show
the same kind of pattern.

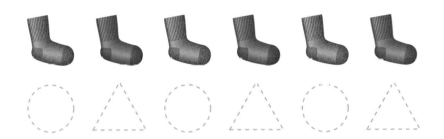

The socks
make a color pattern.
It is red, blue,
red, blue, red,
blue.

Guided Practice

Think
This pattern has
3 things that
repeat.

Find the pattern.
Draw shapes to show it another way.

1.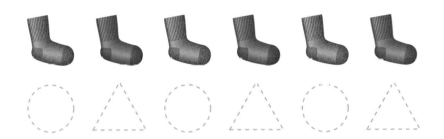

2.

Explain Your Thinking Look at Exercise 2.
How do you decide how many shapes to draw?

Look for the
unit that repeats.

Find the pattern.
Draw shapes to show it another way.

1.

2.

3.

Algebra Readiness ▶ Patterns

4. Use words to tell about the pattern. ↑ ↓ ↑ ↓ ↑ ↓

5. Now use your arms to show the same pattern.

6. **Talk About It** The arrows are a way to show the pattern. What else did we use to show the pattern?

At Home Make a simple repeating pattern.
Have your child show it another way.

Symmetry

 Audio Tutor 1 / 28 Listen and Understand

Objective
Make and identify symmetrical shapes and lines of symmetry.

Vocabulary
symmetry
line of symmetry

Some shapes have **symmetry.**

2 matching parts

Some shapes do not have symmetry.

no matching parts

Follow these steps to make a shape with symmetry.

Step 1

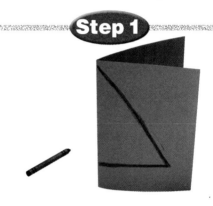

Fold a sheet of paper. Draw a shape.

Step 2

Cut out the shape. Open it.

Step 3

Draw a line on the fold. This is a **line of symmetry.**

Guided Practice

Listen to your teacher.
Draw a line of symmetry.

1.

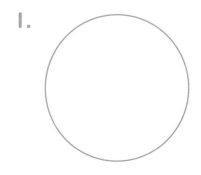

Think
Fold the circle down the middle. Do the 2 parts match?

2.

Explain Your Thinking How did you fold the square to make matching parts? What new shape did you make?

The 2 parts
must match.

Draw a line of symmetry.

1.

2.

3.

4.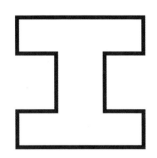

5.

6.

7.

8.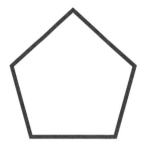

9.

10.

11.

12.

Go on

Name_____

Anna's class takes a walk around the school.
They look for objects with lines of symmetry.

Draw the line of symmetry.
Cross out objects that do not have a line of symmetry.

13. Anna sees a leaf.

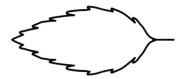

14. Alba finds a feather.

15. Mr. Lai sees a butterfly.

16. Henri sees a gate.

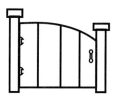

17. Emma sees a game.

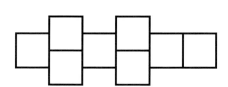

18. Max sees a tree.

19. Lin sees a window.

20. Lois also sees a window.

At Home Take a walk and ask your child to identify objects that have lines of symmetry.

Now Try This Same Size, Same Shape

Some objects are the
same size and shape.

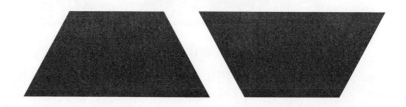

Color the shapes that are the same size and shape.

1.

2.

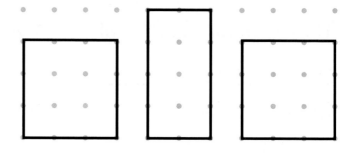

Draw a shape that is the same size and shape.

3.

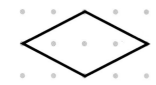

Objects that are the same shape
but different sizes are similar.
Have a classmate draw a shape.
Now draw a shape that is similar.

4.

Name_____

Find a Pattern

Ms. Powers is making this quilt.
You can see the pattern.
What comes next in the pattern?

UNDERSTAND

What do you know?

· The pattern is made with **3** shapes.
· The pattern unit repeats.

PLAN

What is the pattern unit?

You can write the
pattern unit with words.

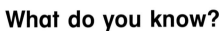

___heart___   ___star___   ___sun___

SOLVE

Circle the one that comes next.

LOOK BACK

Say the pattern.
Does the shape you picked fit the pattern?

Guided Practice

Remember:
► Understand
► Plan
► Solve
► Look Back

Find the pattern to solve.

1. Anita puts this pattern on a shirt.
Circle the shape that comes next.

Think
The pattern unit is X O.

2. Brian sees this pattern on a belt. Put an
X on the shape that is wrong in the pattern.
Draw the correct shape above the X.

Think
The pattern unit is circle, circle, triangle.

Practice

3. Jin is putting this pattern on a blanket.
Circle the shape that comes next in the pattern.

4. Monica sees this pattern on a ribbon. Put an
X on the shape that is wrong in the pattern.
Draw the correct shape above the X.

Go on ▶

Name_____

Mixed Problem Solving

Strategies
Find a Pattern
Draw a Picture
Act It Out With Models
Write a Number Sentence

Solve.

1. Nina makes this pattern on leather. Put an X on the shape that is wrong. Draw the correct shape above the X.

Draw or write to explain.

leather

2. Shani makes 3 pin wheels. Jesse makes 4 pin wheels. How many pin wheels do they make in all?

pin wheel

_____ pin wheels

3. Joan makes a banner. The pattern she makes uses 5 triangles and 5 squares. How many shapes are in her pattern?

banner

_____ shapes

4. **Multistep** Dan makes 4 pot holders. Carmen takes 2 pot holders. Then she gives 1 back. How many pot holders does Dan have now?

pot holder

_____ pot holders

At Home Use 3 shapes to draw a repeating pattern.
Ask your child to describe the pattern and tell what comes next.

Problem Solving on Tests • Listening Skills

Listen to your teacher read the problem.
Solve.

1. Larry saw this dot pattern on a plate.
Use numbers to show the same pattern.

_____ _____ _____ _____ _____ _____

2. Jody sees this pattern on a banner.
Circle what comes next in the pattern.

Listen to your teacher read the problem.
Choose the correct answer.

3.

   ○   ○   ○   ○

4.

   ○   ○   ○   ○

232 two hundred thirty-two

Education Place
See **eduplace.com/map**
for more Test-Taking Tips.

Name_____

This design has symmetry.
The parts on both sides of the line match.

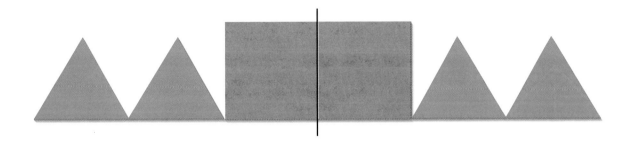

Draw a line of symmetry.

1.

2.

3.

Science Connection
Flower Patterns

Look at the window box.
There are red tulips and yellow tulips.
They make a pattern.

What color tulip comes next in the pattern? _____

Key Topic Review

Bar Graphs

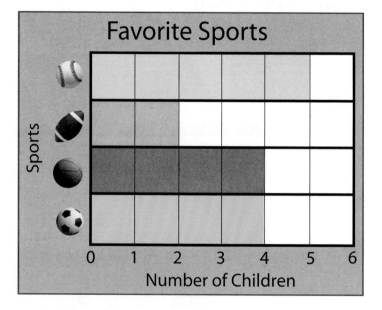

Favorite Sports

Use the bar graph. Solve.

1. How many kinds of sports are on the graph? _____ sports

2. How many children choose ? _____ children

3. How many children choose ? _____ children

4. Circle the sport more children choose.

5. Circle the sport fewer children choose.

Extra Practice at **eduplace.com/map**

Chapter Review/Test

Vocabulary

between	right	left

Fill in the blank with the correct word.

1. The red car is to the _____ of the bus.

2. The bus is _____ the red car and the taxi.

Concepts and Skills

Circle the answer that completes the sentence.

3. The boy is _____ the tree.

   in front of   behind

4. The dog is _____ the cat.

   near   behind

Follow the directions.
Draw an object on the grid.

	Go Right	Go Up	Draw
5.	2 spaces	1 space	🐢
6.	1 space	2 spaces	🦋
7.	1 space	1 space	🌼

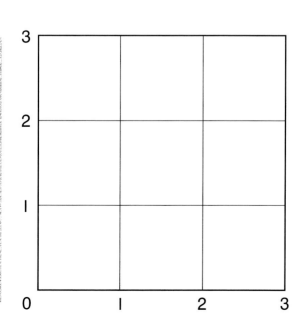

Draw to show a flip.

8.

Draw to show a slide.

9.

Circle the one that comes next.

10.

Use shapes to make a pattern.
Draw the pattern.

11.

Draw a line of symmetry.

12.

13.

14.

Problem Solving

15. Find the pattern to solve.
Trina sees this pattern on a
blanket. Circle the shape that
comes next in the pattern.

Draw or write to explain.

Fractions and Probability

INVESTIGATION

Which picture shows the paper folded in half?

If you folded the paper in half again, how many parts would there be?

✔️ How Many Parts?

First, fold a square piece of paper in half.

Open the paper. How many parts are there?   _____ parts

Next, fold the paper in half two times.

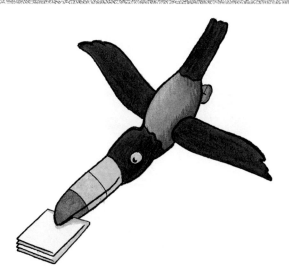

Open the paper. How many parts are there?   _____ parts

Finally, fold the paper in half three times.
Predict how many parts there will be, then open it.

How many parts are there?   _____ parts

Was your prediction correct?   _____

Name_____

Equal Parts

 Audio Tutor 1/29 Listen and Understand

Objective
Identify and count equal parts.

Vocabulary
equal parts

Some whole shapes can be folded into **equal parts.**
Equal parts are the same size.

whole | equal parts | equal parts | equal parts

Guided Practice

Circle the shape that shows equal parts.

1.

Think
Are the 4 parts the same size?

2.

3.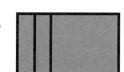

Write the number of equal parts.

4.

_____ equal parts

5.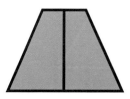

_____ equal parts

6.

_____ equal parts

Explain Your Thinking Look at the rectangle in Exercise 3.
Explain why the shape does not show 3 equal parts.

Practice

Circle the shape that shows equal parts.

Look for parts that are the same size.

1.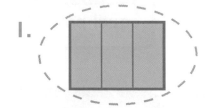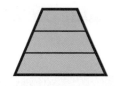

2.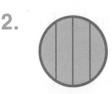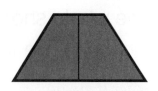

Write the number of equal parts.

3.

__2__ equal parts

4.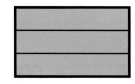

_____ equal parts

5.

_____ equal parts

6.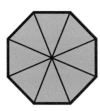

_____ equal parts

7.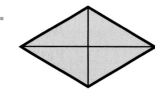

_____ equal parts

8.

_____ equal parts

Problem Solving ▶ Visual Thinking

Draw lines to show the number of equal parts.

9. whole   **2** equal parts   **3** equal parts   **4** equal parts

At Home During a meal, ask your child to name foods that can be cut into equal parts.

One Half

Fractions name equal parts of a whole.

Objective
Use fractions to name parts of a whole; identify one half of a whole.

Vocabulary
fraction   halves   one half

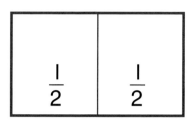

There are **2** equal parts.

There are two **halves.**

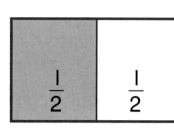

I out of **2** parts is blue.

$\frac{1}{2}$ is blue.

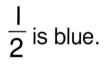
one half

Guided Practice

Think
Look for 2 equal parts.

Circle the shape that shows two halves.

1.

2.

3.

4.

Color $\frac{1}{2}$.

5.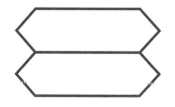

6.

7.

Explain Your Thinking Does it matter which part of the heart you shaded in Exercise 7? Why?

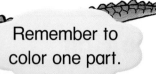

Remember to color one part.

Color $\frac{1}{2}$.

1.

2.

3.

4.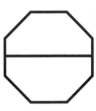

5.

6.

Draw a line to show halves.

Color $\frac{1}{2}$.

7.

8.

9.

Problem Solving ▶ Visual Thinking

10. Rita and Jerome share this apple. Draw a line to show **2** equal parts. Color Rita's part ▬▬▶.

Complete the sentence with numbers.

11. _____ out of _____ parts is red.

12. **Talk About It** Look at the red part. What fraction can you use to tell about it?

At Home Help your child cut a sandwich into two halves and use a fraction to describe each part.

One Fourth

One fourth is a fraction that
names part of a whole.

Objective
Identify one fourth and
one third of a whole.

Vocabulary
fourths   one fourth
thirds   one third

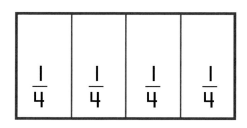

There are **4** equal parts.

There are four **fourths.**

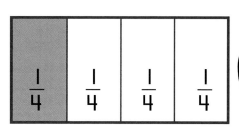

1 out of **4** parts is blue.

$\frac{1}{4}$ is blue.

Guided Practice

Circle the shape that shows four fourths.

Think
Are there 4 equal parts?

1.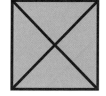

2.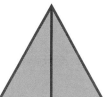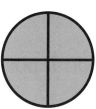

Color $\frac{1}{4}$.

3.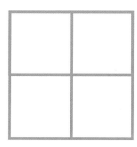

4.

5.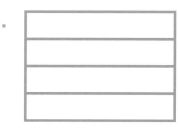

Explain Your Thinking Look at the circle in Exercise 1.
How could you show fourths?

Color the $\frac{1}{4}$.

Color 1 of the 4 parts.

1.
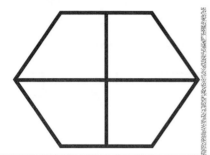

2.
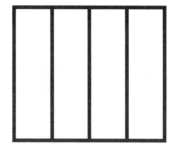

3.
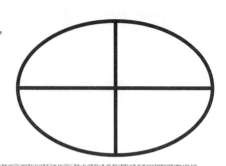

Draw lines to show fourths.

Color $\frac{1}{4}$.

4.
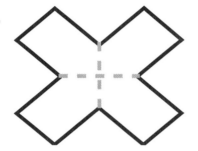

5.
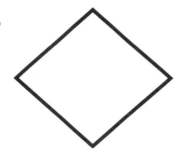

6.

Problem Solving ▶ Visual Thinking

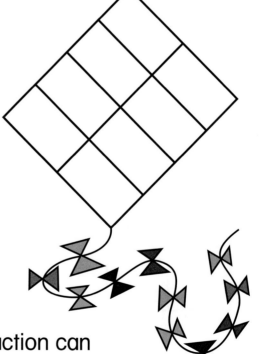

7. Color 1 part of the kite 🖍.

   Color 7 parts of the kite 🖍.

Complete the sentence with numbers.

8. _____ out of _____ parts is yellow.

   _____ out of _____ parts are green.

9. **Talk About It** Look at the kite. What fraction can you use to tell about the green part?

244 two hundred forty-four

At Home Provide various paper shapes and ask your child to show you how to fold paper into fourths.

Go on ➡

Name_____

Now Try This **One Third**

A shape can have **3** equal parts called thirds.

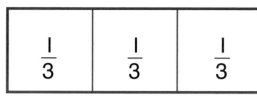 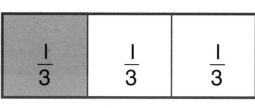 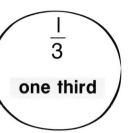

one third

There are **3** equal parts in the whole.

There are three **thirds.**

1 out of **3** parts is blue.

$\frac{1}{3}$ is blue.

Color $\frac{1}{3}$.

1.

2.

3.

Color **1** part. Circle the fraction.

4.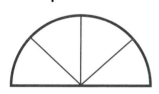

$\frac{1}{2}$ $\frac{1}{3}$ $\frac{1}{4}$

5.

$\frac{1}{2}$ $\frac{1}{3}$ $\frac{1}{4}$

6.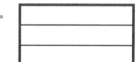

$\frac{1}{2}$ $\frac{1}{3}$ $\frac{1}{4}$

Color **1** part. Write the fraction.

7.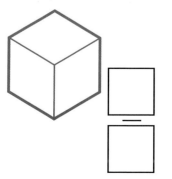

8.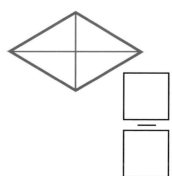

9.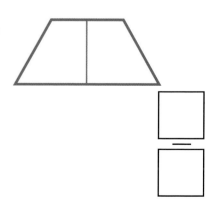

10. **Talk About It** Look at Exercises 7, 8, and 9. Tell what the fraction means for each one.

Write the number of equal parts.

1. 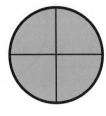   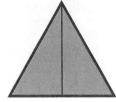

_____ equal parts   _____ equal parts   _____ equal parts

Draw a line to show halves.

Color $\frac{1}{2}$.

2.    3.    4.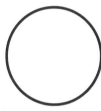

Color $\frac{1}{4}$.

5. 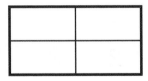   6.    7.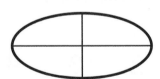

Color $\frac{1}{3}$.

8. 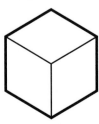   9.    10.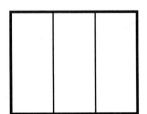

Facts Practice, see page 671

Name_____

Fractions of a Set

Objective

Identify and represent part of a set ($\frac{1}{2}$, $\frac{1}{3}$, $\frac{1}{4}$).

Use a fraction to name a part of a set.

$\frac{1}{4}$ part green
parts in all

Guided Practice

Circle the fraction that names the green part.

1.

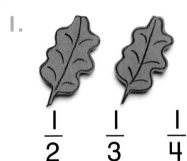

$\frac{1}{2}$ $\frac{1}{3}$ $\frac{1}{4}$

Think
2 parts in all.
I part is green.

2.

$\frac{1}{2}$ $\frac{1}{3}$ $\frac{1}{4}$

3.

$\frac{1}{2}$ $\frac{1}{3}$ $\frac{1}{4}$

4.

$\frac{1}{2}$ $\frac{1}{3}$ $\frac{1}{4}$

Color to show the fraction.

5. $\frac{1}{3}$

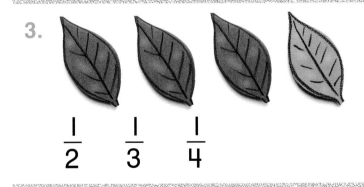

6. $\frac{1}{4}$

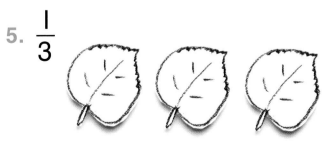

Explain Your Thinking Look at Exercise 4. What does the fraction $\frac{1}{2}$ tell you about the leaves?

Look for one part of the set.

Circle the fraction that names the green part.

1.

$\dfrac{1}{2}$ $\dfrac{1}{3}$ $\dfrac{1}{4}$

2.

$\dfrac{1}{2}$ $\dfrac{1}{3}$ $\dfrac{1}{4}$

Color to show the fraction.

3. $\dfrac{1}{4}$

4. $\dfrac{1}{3}$

Problem Solving ▶ Reasoning

5. Zack draws a tree with 4 apples.
   Color 3 of the apples ▬▬▬▶.
   Color 1 of the apples ▬▬▬▶.

Complete the sentence.
Write the fraction.

6. _____ out of _____ apples is green.

7. _____ out of _____ apples are red.

At Home Use a collection of like items to make sets of 2, 3, and 4.
Ask your child to use a fraction to identify one item in each set.

Name_____

Activity: Probability

 Audio Tutor I/31 Listen and Understand

Work Together

Predict what will happen when you spin a spinner. Then check your predictions.

> **Objective**
> Predict and determine the probability of an event.
>
> predict   certain
> impossible   probable

Step 1

Predict What do you think will happen when you spin each spinner?

Spinner A

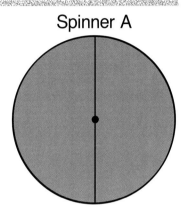

- **Spinner A**

  It is **certain** that it will point to ____blue____.

- **Spinner B**

  It is **impossible** that it will point to ____blue____.

Spinner B

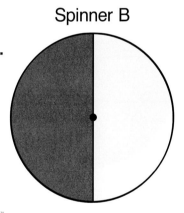

- **Spinner C**

  It is **probable** that it will point to ____blue____.

Step 2

Spin Use Spinner C. Spin 10 times.
Record your spins in the tally chart.

Spinner C

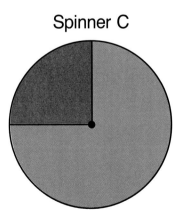

1.

Spins	
■	
■	

2. **Talk About It** Which color did you land on more often? Why?

On Your Own

Look at Spinner B. Predict.

1. Are you certain to spin red?

   Spinner B

   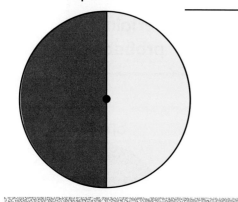

   _____

2. Use a paper clip and a pencil. Spin 10 times. Record your spins in the tally chart.

Spins	
⬜	
⬛	

Look at Spinner D. Predict.

3. Are you certain to spin red?

   Spinner D

   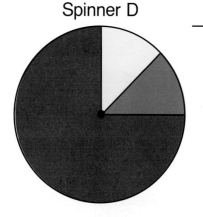

   _____

4. Try It. Spin 10 times. Record your spins in the tally chart.

Spins	
⬛	
⬜	
🟥	

5. On which spinner is it impossible to spin blue? _____

Will it happen? Draw a line to match.

6. A lion will put you to bed.    certain

7. You will go to school today.   probable

8. A fish will swim.   impossible

 At Home Think of some familiar events. Ask your child to identify each as certain, probable, or impossible.

250 two hundred fifty

Go on

Name _____

Keesha's bag has 🔲 🔲 🔲 🔲 .
She will pick one cube.

She is **more likely** to pick 🔲 .

She is **less likely** to pick 🔲 .

Tu's bag has 🔲 🔲 🔲 🔲 .
He will pick one cube.

He is **equally likely** to pick 🔲
as 🔲 .

How likely is it that you will pick blue? Circle.

1.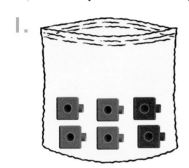

more likely

equally likely

less likely

2.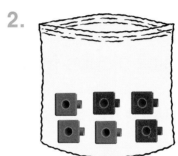

more likely

equally likely

less likely

3.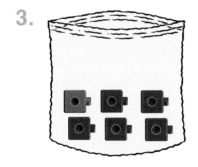

more likely

equally likely

less likely

4.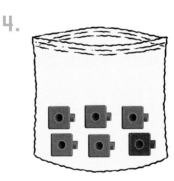

more likely

equally likely

less likely

When there are more than **2** colors, you need
to say **most likely** and **least likely**.
How likely is it that you will pick blue? Circle.

5.

most likely

least likely

6.

most likely

least likely

Game

Fair or Unfair?

2 Players

What You Need:

Bag with ⬛ ⬛ ⬛ and ⬛ ⬛ ⬛ ,

Bag with ⬛ ⬛ ⬛ ⬛ ⬛ and ⬛ , ten frame (LT2),

red and blue crayons

How to Play

1. Each player takes a bag and a ten frame.

2. You each pick a cube from your bag.

3. Color 1 square the same color as the cube.

4. Put the cube back in the bag.

5. Keep playing until both players color all their squares.

6. The player with more blue than red wins.

Talk About It Look inside your bag. Who is more likely to win? Is the game fair?

Name _____

Use a Picture

Manny has a bag of cubes.
He asks Hannah to pick
a cube from the bag.

Objective
Use data from a picture
to solve problems.

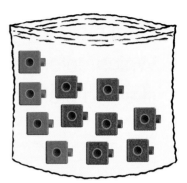
Manny's bag

You can use a picture to predict the chance of something happening.

Is Hannah more likely to pick a red cube
or a blue cube?

_____red_____ cube

Think
There are more
red cubes than
blue cubes.

You can use a picture to compare groups.

How many more red cubes than blue cubes
does Manny have in his bag?

_____ ◯ _____ = _____

_____ more red cubes

Think
I count 7 red cubes
and 4 blue cubes. I can
subtract to find how many
more red cubes
there are.

Use the picture to solve.

1. Gina picks a marble from the bag. Which color marble is she more likely to pick?

Draw or write to explain.

Think
I count 8 red and 3 blue.

_____

2. Gina compares the red and blue marbles in her bag. How many more red marbles than blue marbles does she have?

Think
I can subtract 8 − 3 to find how many more red marbles she has.

_____ more red marbles

Practice

3. Sam asks Jamal to pick a button from his bag. Which color button is he more likely to pick?

_____

4. Sam compares the red and blue buttons in his bag. How many more blue buttons than red buttons does he have?

_____ more blue buttons

Name_____

Mixed Problem Solving

Strategies
Find a Pattern
Act It Out With Models
Write a Number Sentence

Solve.

1. Lynn asks Carlos to pick a checker. Which color checker is he more likely to pick?

Draw or write to explain.

checkers

_____

2. Nita is making this pattern on a quilt. Circle the color that comes next in the pattern.

red

yellow

blue

quilt

3. **Multistep** Marta picks up 2 jacks and puts them in a pile. She picks up 2 more jacks. Then she loses 1 jack. How many jacks are in her pile now?

jacks

_____ jacks

Use the tally chart to solve the problem.

4. How many origami birds does Nita make?

Animals Made	
birds	JHT I
frogs	III
bugs	JHT

_____ birds

At Home Put two colors of like objects in a bag as shown in the lesson. Ask your child to predict which color he or she is more likely to pick. Take turns picking and returning the object to bag.

Problem Solving on Tests • Listening Skills

Open Response

Listen to your teacher read the problem.
Use the picture to solve.

Show your work using pictures, numbers, or words.

1. Pretend it is your turn to pick a cube from the bag. Which color are you more likely to pick?

_____

2. Compare the cubes in the bag. How many more gray cubes than white cubes are in there?

_____ more gray cubes

Multiple Choice

Listen to your teacher read the problem.
Choose the correct answer.

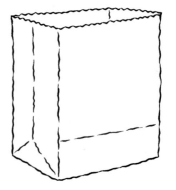

3.   red   blue   yellow   green
          ○   ○   ○   ○

4.   red   blue   yellow   green
          ○   ○   ○   ○

Education Place
See eduplace.com/map
for more Test-Taking Tips.

Name_____

Now Try This **Predict and Spin**

Predict how many times you will get each color in 10 spins.

Then, check your prediction by spinning and recording your results.

Think
Which color might you land on most often?

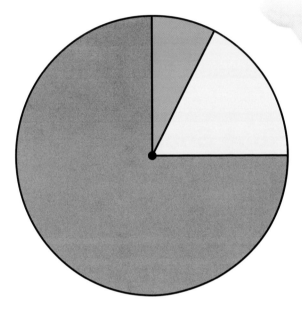

Color	Predict the Number	Tally the 10 spins
yellow		
orange		
green		
	Total: 10	Total: 涉涉涉涉涉 涉涉涉涉涉

Art Connection
Shape Painting

Some pictures are made up of shapes.

What shape do you see in this picture? _____

How many can you find? _____

painting by Bruce Gray

WEEKLY WR READER eduplace.com/map

Key Topic Review Plane Shapes

Trace the shape.
Write how many sides and corners.

1. triangle

_____ sides

_____ corners

2. rectangle

_____ sides

_____ corners

3. circle

_____ sides

_____ corners

4. square

_____ sides

_____ corners

Extra Practice at **eduplace.com/map**

Chapter Review/Test

Vocabulary

1. Draw a line to match.

one fourth

$\frac{1}{3}$

one third

$\frac{1}{2}$

one half

$\frac{1}{4}$

Concepts and Skills

Write the number of equal parts.

2.

_____ equal parts

3.
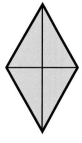
_____ equal parts

4.
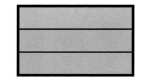
_____ equal parts

Color $\frac{1}{4}$.

5.
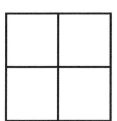

Color $\frac{1}{2}$.

6.
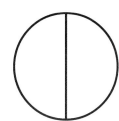

Color $\frac{1}{3}$.

7.

Color to show the fraction.

8. $\frac{1}{2}$

9. $\frac{1}{4}$

Will it happen?
Draw a line to match.

10. The sun shines on you at night.   certain

11. You sing during music time.   probable

12. Puppies will grow.   impossible

How likely is it that you will pick red?
Circle.

13.    more likely

equally likely

less likely

14.    more likely

equally likely

less likely

Problem Solving
Use the picture to solve.

15. Dom picks a marble from the
bag. Which color marble is he
more likely to pick?

Draw or write to explain.

_____

Name_____

Growing Patterns

Look at the picture.
Count and write the number of squares.
Draw and write what comes next.

1.

2   4   6

_____

2.

1   3   6

_____

3.

 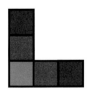

___ ___ ___

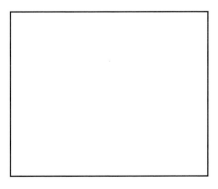

_____

Education Place
Visit **eduplace.com/map**
for brain teasers.

Computer
Modeling Fractions

Use the fraction models found at
eduplace.com/map to show fractions.

1. Set the number of equal parts.
   - Put your pointer over the **scissors.**
   - Choose how many equal parts you want.
   - Click on a fraction circle.

2. Shade the fraction.
   - Click **Fill.**
   - Click a section of the circle.

3. Click **[1 2 3]**

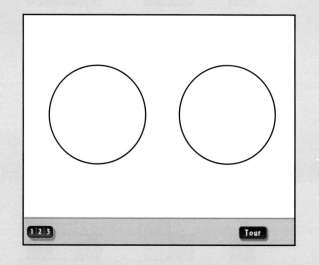

Use the fraction models to show each fraction.
Draw each fraction.

1. Show $\frac{1}{3}$.

2. Show $\frac{1}{4}$.

3. Show $\frac{1}{2}$.

Vocabulary

Match the word to the correct shape.

1.   **cylinder**

2.   **sphere**

3.   **cone**

Concepts and Skills

Circle one way the objects are alike.

4.

color

size

shape

Trace the shape.
Write the number of sides and corners.

5. square

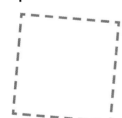

_____ sides

_____ corners

6. triangle

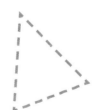

_____ sides

_____ corners

Read the sorting rule.
Circle the solid shapes that follow the rule.

7. All faces

Unit 3 Test

Look at the grid.

Write your own directions.

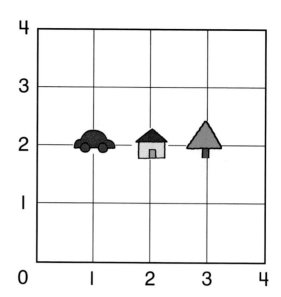

8. Tell how to get to the tree.

   Go right _____ spaces.

   Go up _____ spaces.

Complete the sentence.

9. The house is _____ the car and the tree.

Draw to show a flip.

10.

Draw a line of symmetry.

11.

Use any shapes to make a pattern.
Draw the pattern.

12.

Color $\frac{1}{2}$.

13.

Color to show the fraction.

14. $\frac{1}{4}$

Problem Solving

15. Wes sees this pattern. Put an X on the shape that is wrong. Draw the correct shape above the X.

264 two hundred sixty-four

Test-Taking Tips

· ·

Check your work when you have finished all of the problems.

Reread each problem to make sure you have answered the question.

Multiple Choice

Fill in the ○ for the correct answer.

1. Which shape is a triangle?

○   ○   ○   ○

3. Which solid has 5 faces, 8 edges, and 5 corners?

○   ○   ○   ○

2. Use the bar graph. How many children like winter best?

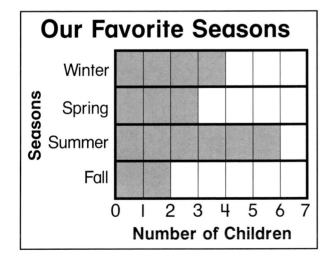

Our Favorite Seasons

Number of Children

3   4   5   6

○   ○   ○   ○

4. Which kite has 4 equal parts?

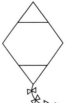         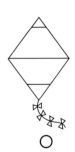

○   ○   ○   ○

Fill in the ○ for the correct answer. NH means not here.

5. Which rectangle shows thirds?

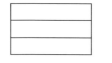

○   ○   ○

6. There are **6** turtles on a log. Then **2** more turtles come. How many turtles are there in all?

6   7   8   9
○   ○   ○   ○

7. There are **8** bananas in a bunch. Joe eats **2**. How many bananas are left?

2   4   6   NH
○   ○   ○   ○

Solve.

8. Draw the next two shapes in this pattern.

_____   _____

9. What number do these tally marks show?

_____

10. Ali, Ana, Gina, and Ted use this spinner to play a game. What number are they most likely to spin?

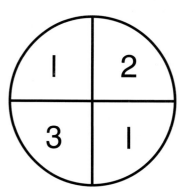

_____

![Education Place] **Education Place**
Look for Cumulative Test Prep at
eduplace.com/map for more practice.

266 two hundred sixty-six

UNIT 4

Party Under the Sea

written by Laura Black
illustrated by Janet Skiles

READING MATH

Skip Count Sea

Look back at the story to answer these questions.

▲ 1. Look at page 4. Skip count by 2s to count the dancers.

▲ 2. Look at page 6. Count how many arms there are on 3 starfish.

★ 3. Look at page 7. What if there are 5 more fish? Continue counting to find how many sea friends there are.

☐ 4. Look at page 7. How would you count how many eyes there are on the 5 blue crabs?

Answers
1. 12   2. 5, 10, 15   3. 26, 27, 28, 29, 30
4. Possible answer: I would skip count by 2s to get 10 eyes altogether.

Reading Strategies	
▲ Noting Details	★ Predict ☐ Evaluate

8

The fish are having a party.

They're inviting us to come.

Why don't we join them

For some counting fun?

Finish counting the fish: 1, 2, ▮, ▮.

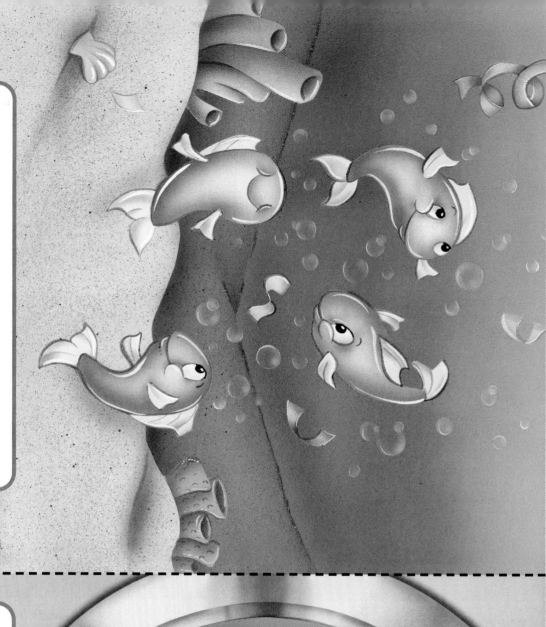

Now the day is over.

We're all so glad we came.

We hope that you had fun

Playing the counting game.

Finish counting the sea friends: 22, 23, ▮, ▮.

7

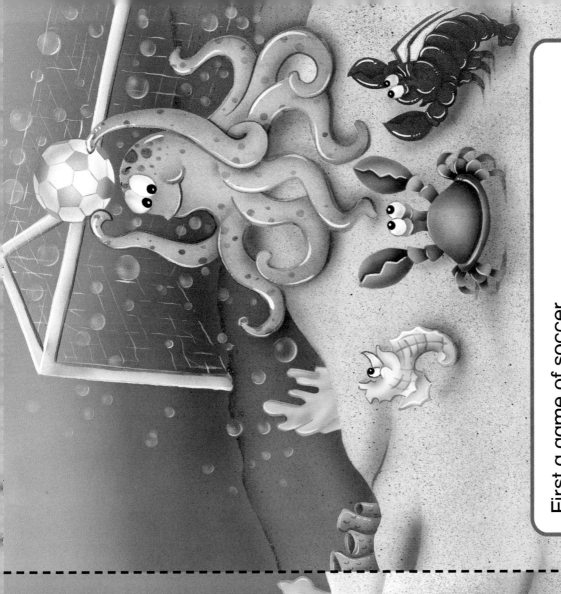

First a game of soccer.

The octopus can't be beat!

I wonder if it's because

She has so many feet!

Finish counting the octopus feet: 5, 6, ▢, ▢.

The starfish form a mountain

With a flag on the top.

Quickly start to count them

Before they all go FLOP!

Finish counting the starfish: 17, 18, ▢, ▢.

The catfish and dogfish are dancing.

I've never seen this before!

How many dancers do you see

Out on the big dance floor?

Finish counting the dancers: 9, 10, ▢, ▢.

Some seals all got together

And started a big sack race.

Be careful when you count them

So you don't lose your place!

Finish counting the seals: 13, 14, ▢, ▢.

5